THE CIVIL RIGHTS MOVEMENT

ENZO GEORGE

Cavendish Square

New York

Published in 2016 by Cavendish Square Publishing, LLC
243 5th Avenue, Suite 136, New York, NY 10016

© 2016 Brown Bear Books Ltd

First Edition

Website: cavendishsq.com

This publication represents the opinions and views of the author based on his or her personal experiences, knowledge, and research. The information in this book serves as a general guide only. the author and publisher have used their best efforts in preparing this book and disclaim liability rising directly or indirectly from the use and application of this book.

CPSIA Compliance Information: Batch #WS15CSQ

All websites were available and accurate when this book was sent to press.

Library of Congress Cataloging-in-Publication Data

George, Enzo.
The Civil Rights Movement / by Enzo George.
     p. cm. — (Primary sources in U.S. history)
Includes index.
ISBN 978-1-50260-496-5 (hardcover) ISBN 978-1-50260-497-2 (ebook)
1. African Americans — Civil rights — History — 20th century — Juvenile literature. 2. Civil rights movements — United States — History — 20th century — Juvenile literature. 3. United States — Race relations — Juvenile literature. I. George, Enzo. II. Title.
E185.61 G47 2016
323.1196'073—d23

For Brown Bear Books Ltd:
Editorial Director: Lindsey Lowe
Managing Editor: Tim Cooke
Children's Publisher: Anne O'Daly
Design Manager: Keith Davis
Designer: Lynne Lennon
Picture Manager: Sophie Mortimer

Picture Credits:
Front Cover : center right © Corbis/Bettman; bottom © Getty Images/Francis Miller/Time Life Pictures.
All images © Library of Congress, except; 21, 22, 25 © Alamy/Everett Collection; 31 © Corbis/Bettmann, 41 © Corbis/ Flip Schulke, 34 © Corbis/Fred Ward; 19 © CMRVET; 9, 12, 16, 40, 43 © Robert Hunt Library.

Brown Bear Books has made every attempt to contact the copyright holder.
If you have any information please contact licensing@brownbearbooks.co.uk

We believe the extracts included in this book to be material in the public domain.
Anyone having further information should contact licensing@brownbearbooks.co.uk

Manufactured in the United States of America

CONTENTS

INTRODUCTION

Primary sources are the best way to get close to people from the past. They include the things people wrote in diaries, letters, or books; the paintings, drawings, maps, or cartoons they created; and even the buildings they constructed, the clothes they wore, or the possessions they owned. Such sources often reveal a lot about how people saw themselves and how they thought about their world.

This book collects a range of primary sources from the campaign for civil rights from the late 1940s until the late 1960s, when black Americans claimed their constitutional rights through legal cases supported by nonviolent protest.

African Americans had long claimed equal rights, but more urgent calls for an end to racial segregation followed World War II (1939–1945). In the 1950s, civil rights organizations emerged under inspirational leaders, such as Reverend Martin Luther King, Jr. Their calls for desegregation gained widespread support, but in the South local and state authorities blocked change with violence. Eventually, mass action and the use of federal force to administer civil rights laws brought change in the 1960s. For some African Americans, however, the change was too little and too slow. The late 1960s saw race riots and the emergence of more aggressive African American groups.

HOW TO USE THIS BOOK

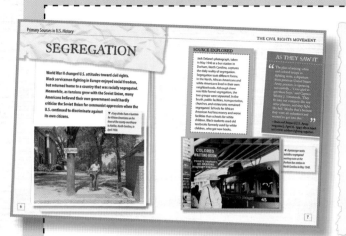

Each spread contains at least one primary source. Look out for "Source Explored" boxes that explain images from the civil rights struggle, who made them, and why. There are also "As They Saw It" boxes that contain quotes from people of the period.

Some boxes contain more detailed information about a particular aspect of a subject. The subjects are arranged in roughly chronological order. They focus on key events or people. There is a full timeline of the period at the back of the book.

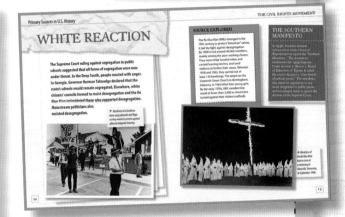

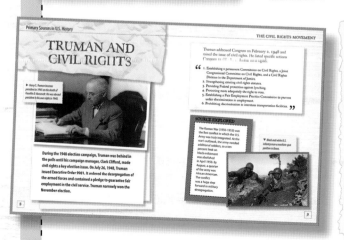

Some spreads feature a longer extract from a contemporary eyewitness. Look for the colored introduction that explains who the writer is and the origin of his or her account. These accounts are often accompanied by a related visual primary source.

SEGREGATION

World War II changed U.S. attitudes toward civil rights. Black servicemen fighting in Europe enjoyed social freedom, but returned home to a country that was still racially segregated. Meanwhile, as tensions grew with the Soviet Union, many Americans believed their own government could hardly criticize the Soviet Union for communist oppression when the U.S. continued to discriminate against its own citizens.

▼ *A boy drinks from a fountain for African Americans on the lawn of the county courthouse in Halifax, North Carolina, in April 1938.*

SOURCE EXPLORED

Jack Delano's photograph, taken in May 1940 at a bus station in Durham, North Carolina, captures the daily reality of segregation. Segregation took different forms. In the North, African Americans and white Americans lived in their own neighborhoods. Although there was little formal segregation, the two groups were separated. In the South, public facilities, transportation, churches, and restaurants remained segregated. Schools for African American had less money and worse facilities than schools for white children. Black students used old textbooks formerly used by white children, who got new books.

AS THEY SAW IT

" The plan of mixing white and colored troops in fighting units, a departure from previous United States Army practice, is operating successfully... 'I was glad to get those boys,' said Captain Wesley J. Simmonds. 'They fit into our company like any other platoon, and they fight like hell. Maybe that's because they were all volunteers and wanted to get into this.' "

—*Stars and Stripes* (U.S. Army magazine), April 6, 1945, about black and white soldiers fighting together

◀ *A passenger waits outside a segregated waiting room at the Durham bus station in North Carolina in May 1940.*

TRUMAN AND CIVIL RIGHTS

▶ Harry S. Truman became president in 1945 after the death of Franklin D. Roosevelt. He was elected president in his own right in 1948.

During the 1948 election campaign, Truman was behind in the polls until his campaign manager, Clark Clifford, made civil rights a key election issue. On July 26, 1948, Truman issued Executive Order 9981. It ordered the desegregation of the armed forces and contained a pledge to guarantee fair employment in the civil service. Truman narrowly won the November election.

Truman addressed Congress on February 2, 1948, and raised the issue of civil rights. He listed specific actions Congress could take to further civil rights:

" 1. Establishing a permanent Commission on Civil Rights, a Joint Congressional Committee on Civil Rights, and a Civil Rights Division in the Department of Justice.
2. Strengthening existing civil rights statutes.
3. Providing Federal protection against lynching.
4. Protecting more adequately the right to vote.
5. Establishing a Fair Employment Practice Commission to prevent unfair discrimination in employment.
6. Prohibiting discrimination in interstate transportation facilities. **"**

SOURCE EXPLORED

The Korean War (1950–1953) was the first conflict in which the U.S. Army was truly integrated. At the war's outbreak, the army needed additional soldiers, so a 10 percent limit on black enlistment was abolished in April 1950. By August, a quarter of the army was African American. The conflict was a huge step forward in military desegregation.

▼ Black and white U.S. infantry man a machine-gun position in Korea.

BROWN v. BOARD OF EDUCATION

▲ Girls share an integrated high-school class at Anacostia High School in Washington, D.C., in September 1957.

Linda Brown, an African-American third-grader in Topeka, Kansas, walked a mile each morning to an all-black elementary school. An all-white school seven blocks from her house refused to accept her as a student. In December 1952, President Truman ordered the Justice Department to support the family against the Kansas Board of Education in the Supreme Court. On May 17, 1954, the Supreme Court ruled in *Brown v. Board of Education of Topeka* that segregating public schools was unconstitutional.

◀ *Black students arrive at Clinton High School on December 4, 1956. The day was marked by violence that forced the school to shut for a week.*

SOURCE EXPLORED

Black students walk through white students as they arrive at Clinton High School, Tennessee, in December 1956. Clinton was the first high school in the South to be integrated following the Supreme Court ruling in *Brown v. Board of Education*. An 1896 court decision—*Plessy v. Ferguson*—had ruled in favor of "separate but equal" education. The new ruling declared that separate education went against the Fourteenth Amendment, which gives equal protection to all citizens. Clinton High School was forced to close on December 4, 1956, but reopened six days later as an integrated school.

LEGAL LEADER

The Brown family lawyer in *Brown v. Board of Education* was Thurgood Marshall. Marshall was a leader of the movement to achieve civil rights by working through the courts. He also founded and worked for the Legal Defense and Educational Fund of the National Association for the Advancement of Colored People (NAACP), the leading civil rights organization. In 1967 Marshall became the first African-American justice on the U.S. Supreme Court, where he served until 1991.

WHITE REACTION

The Supreme Court ruling against segregation in public schools suggested that all forms of segregation were now under threat. In the Deep South, people reacted with anger. In Georgia, Governor Herman Talmadge declared that the state's schools would remain segregated. Elsewhere, white citizens' councils formed to resist desegregation while the Ku Klux Klan intimidated those who supported desegregation. Mainstream politicians also resisted desegregation.

▼ *Residents of a Southern town carry placards and flags as they march in protest against plans to integrate housing.*

SOURCE EXPLORED

The Ku Klux Klan (KKK) emerged in the nineteenth century to protect "American" values. It led the fight against desegregation. By 1958 it had around forty thousand members. They wore white, hooded robes, carried burning torches, and used violence to further their cause. Between 1958 and 1963, they carried out at least 138 bombings. The attack on the Sixteenth Street Church in Birmingham, Alabama, in 1963 killed four young girls. By the early 1970s, KKK membership stood at fewer than two thousand as Americans turned against the group's violent methods.

THE SOUTHERN MANIFESTO

In 1956, Southern senators and members of the House of Representatives signed the "Southern Manifesto." The declaration condemned the 1954 Supreme Court decision in *Brown v. Board of Education of Topeka*. It called the court's decision a "clear breach of judicial power." The manifesto also stated its opposition to any racial integration in public places and encouraged states to ignore the decision of the Supreme Court.

◀ Members of the Ku Klux Klan burn a cross in a ceremony in Knoxville, Tennessee, in September 1948.

MONTGOMERY BUS BOYCOTT

▶ Rosa Parks sits in a "white" seat on a bus in this reconstruction of her famous refusal to give up her seat to a white passenger.

In Alabama, the law required African-American passengers to sit at the back of a bus and to give up their seat if a white person wanted it. On December 1, 1955, in Montgomery, a forty-two-year-old seamstress named Rosa Parks refused to give up her seat. She was arrested. African-American pastors called on their congregations to boycott the city's buses. The boycott began on December 5 and lasted 381 days. It was one of the most significant protests of the early civil rights movement.

SOURCE EXPLORED

Rosa Parks has her fingerprints taken in this recreation of her arrest. The bus boycott sparked by the arrest lasted for 381 days. In November 1956, the Supreme Court ruled that the Montgomery bus company's policy of segregation violated the U.S. Constitution. The bus company, which had seen its profits plunge, agreed to end segregation on their vehicles and to hire black drivers.

▲ *Rosa Parks became one of the most enduring symbols of the civil rights movement.*

Rosa Parks was a member of the NAACP. Her refusal to give up her seat is sometimes said to have been the result of her being tired, but she said, "The only tired I was, was tired of giving in." Here, she recalls refusing the bus driver's request to give up her seat:

❝ He said, 'Well, I'm going to have you arrested.' I said, 'You may do that.' These were the only words we said to each other... As I sat there, I tried not to think about what might happen. I knew that anything was possible. I could be manhandled or beaten. I could be arrested. People have asked me if it occurred to me that I could be the test case the NAACP had been looking for. I did not think about that at all. In fact if I had let myself think too deeply about what might happen to me, I might have gotten off the bus. But I chose to remain. **❞**

MARTIN LUTHER KING JR.

Martin Luther King Jr. was a pastor in Montgomery, Alabama. His involvement in the 1956 bus boycott caused him to become one of the leaders of the civil rights movement. King came from a well-off family and resented being treated as a second-class citizen because of his color. A devout Christian, he challenged racism through nonviolent actions such as peaceful sit-ins and marches.

▼ King waves to crowds during the March on Washington, August 28, 1963, when he delivered one of his greatest speeches, "I have a dream."

▼ *King preaches in a Baptist church. He came from a long tradition of powerful oratory by African American preachers.*

NONVIOLENCE

Martin Luther King's message of change through nonviolent protest was influenced by the Indian nationalist leader Mahatma Gandhi (1869-1948). Gandhi used nonviolent mass action against India's British rulers to secure independence for the country. Gandhi's tactics included demonstrations, sit-ins, picketing, vigils, fasting and hunger strikes, blockades, and civil disobedience. The goal of nonviolence is to convert the opponent to the right way of thinking.

SOURCE EXPLORED

In this photograph, a young Martin Luther King Jr. is seen preaching in front of a cross inside a church. In 1954, aged just twenty-five and while still finishing his doctoral dissertation, King was appointed pastor of the Dexter Avenue Baptist Church in Montgomery, Alabama. His father, grandfather, and great-grandfather had been pastors before him, and King drew on a tradition of African-American preachers who were also social leaders. Also in the African-American preaching tradition, King was a great orator. His speeches and sermons inspired a generation to believe that change could come. Between 1957 and 1968, King made more than 2,500 speeches. Even while he led the civil rights movement, he continued to preach across the country, drawing huge crowds who wanted to hear him.

CIVIL RIGHTS ORGANIZATIONS

The civil rights movement was organized by a number of groups. The oldest was the National Association for the Advancement of Colored People (NAACP), set up in 1909. In 1942, the Congress of Racial Equality (CORE) was formed to coordinate nonviolent protest. In 1960, African American students founded the Student Nonviolent Coordinating Committee, which also promoted peaceful protest.

▼ Civil rights leaders (left to right): John Lewis, Whitney M. Young Jr., Asa Philip Randolph, Martin Luther King Jr., James Farmer, and Roy Wilkins.

▼ *Civil rights pins had bold designs and simple slogans— and could get their wearers into a lot of trouble in the South.*

THE SCLC

In early 1957, after the Montgomery Bus Boycott, Martin Luther King Jr. and other African-American ministers formed the Southern Christian Leadership Conference (SCLC). Its motto was "To Redeem the Soul of America" and its function was to coordinate local nonviolent protest movements across the South. The SCLC believed African-American churches should lead the struggle for civil rights. To begin with, however, its commitment to nonviolence made it difficult for it to fight its racist opponents and to attract supporters.

SOURCE EXPLORED

All the major civil rights groups produced pins. They were cheap to make and identified the wearer as a supporter of the organization. But, although pins were cheap and small, the price for wearing one could be high, especially in the South. A pin from the NAACP, SCLC, SNCC, or CORE declared its wearer's support for the civil rights movement. African-American wearers of pins in particular ran the risk of being physically or verbally abused by opponents to civil rights. To get the message across, the best pins were the simplest. They featured a strong image—such as the SNCC's pin of a black hand shaking a white hand—and a few words. "We Shall Overcome" was among the most popular phrases used on different pins.

LITTLE ROCK SCHOOL CRISIS

▲ *White citizens march against school integration at the Arkansas State Capitol in Little Rock on August 20, 1959.*

In September 1957, nine African American students arrived at the all-white Central High School in Little Rock, Arkansas. Central High was to be the first integrated school in the state. The Arkansas Governor Orval Faubus, who was seeking reelection, refused to allow the students to enroll. He ordered the Arkansas National Guard to keep them out of the school. President Eisenhower sent in federal troops to protect the students from white onlookers who attacked them outside the school.

◀ *Hazel Massery shouts at Elizabeth Eckford. While the other eight black students arrived together, Eckford arrived on her own to be turned away from the school by the Arkansas National Guard.*

SOURCE EXPLORED

Hazel Bryan Massery screams as Elizabeth Eckford arrives at Little Rock school on September 4, 1957. The Little Rock Nine finally entered the school on September 25, protected by the 101st Airborne Division. In later life, Eckford and Massery reconciled, but fell out again when Eckford claimed Massery still harbored racist views.

Elizabeth Eckford describes being turned away by the Arkansas National Guard on September 4, 1957:

❝ The crowd was quiet. I guess they were waiting to see what was going to happen. When I was able to steady my knees, I walked past the guard who had let the white students in. He didn't move. When I tried to squeeze past him, he raised his bayonet... I was very frightened and didn't know what to do. I turned around and the crowd came toward me. They moved closer and closer. Somebody started yelling, 'Lynch her! Lynch her!' I tried to see a friendly face somewhere in the mob... I looked into the face of an old woman and it seemed a kind face, but when I looked at her again, she spat on me. They came closer, shouting... 'Get out of here!' ❞

NONVIOLENT PROTEST

One of the most visible examples of segregation was the refusal of restaurants, lunch counters, and soda fountains to serve African Americans. On February 1, 1960, four African-American students staged a sit-in at the lunch counter of a Woolworth store in Greensboro, North Carolina. The sit-in was broadcast on TV. Soon college students across the country were staging their own sit-ins in an effort to end segregation.

▼ *Ministers picket a Woolworth store in New York City in February 1960 to protest segregated lunch counters.*

SOURCE EXPLORED

In this photograph, taken on February 2, 1960, three African-American students—from left, Ronald Martin, Robert Patterson, and Mark Martin—sit at the lunch counter of Greensboro's Woolworth store. They followed four freshmen from North Carolina Agricultural and Technical College who had sat at the counter the previous day. When they were refused service, they stayed in their seats until closing time, vowing to return until they were served. From Greensboro, sit-ins spread across the country. Soon, revenue at Woolworth and other restaurants fell so much that store-owners abandoned segregation. On July 25, 1960, the first four freshmen were the first African Americans to be served at the lunch counter in Woolworth in Greensboro.

AS THEY SAW IT

" Spokesmen Franklin McLain and Ezell Blair Jr. stated that the group is seeking luncheon counter service... Blair declared that Negro adults 'have become complacent and fearful.' He declared, 'It is time for someone to wake up and change the situation... and we decided to start here.' McLain said... 'We like to spend our money here, but we want to spend it at the lunch counter as well as the counter next to it. "

–*The Greensboro Record,* February 2, 1960

◀ *Protestors sit at the lunch counter in a Greensboro Woolworth. Many sit-ins were met with violence from whites.*

THE FREEDOM RIDES

Segregation on interstate buses had been ruled illegal by the Supreme Court in 1946. In 1947, however, a racially mixed group of men traveling by bus through the South were attacked. In 1961 volunteers set out on a new series of "freedom rides" through the South. Again, they frequently met with violence from white racists. The Freedom Riders were beaten up or arrested, and their buses were set on fire.

▼ *Freedom Riders watch their bus burn in the aftermath of an attack by white racists in Anniston, Alabama, on May 14, 1961.*

◀ *White volunteers leave Washington, D.C. They planned to arrive in New Orleans on May 17, 1961, the seventh anniversary of the Supreme Court decision in Brown v. Board of Education.*

SOURCE EXPLORED

Protestors hang placards out of a bus as it leaves Washington, D.C., on May 4, 1961. Activists from CORE had decided to stage a new Freedom Ride to New Orleans to test President John F. Kennedy's commitment to civil rights. When the bus arrived in Birmingham, Alabama, on May 14, the Public Safety Commissioner, Eugene "Bull" Connor gave the police the day off. The freedom riders were attacked and beaten up. The same thing happened in Montgomery, Alabama. The riders never reached New Orleans, but the publicity they gained forced Attorney General Robert Kennedy to tighten the 1946 ruling. He forced the integration of interstate buses on November 1, 1961.

AS THEY SAW IT

❝ You could see baseball bats; you could see hammers; you could see pieces of chain. You knew why they were there... And you knew it was very soon going to happen. At that moment... I bowed by head, and I prayed. And I asked God to give me the strength to be nonviolent. I asked God to forgive them for whatever they might do. And I asked Him to be with me. ❞

—White Freedom Rider Jim Zwerg in a lecture from 2002

VIOLENCE IN BIRMINGHAM

In 1963, the Southern Christian Leadership Conference concentrated its protests on Birmingham, Alabama. The police used dogs to attack protestors. Martin Luther King was jailed. On September 15, 1963, racists bombed the Sixteenth Street Baptist Church, killing four young girls. The outraged popular reaction was a turning point in the civil rights movement.

▼ Wrecked trailers mark the site of a bomb attack on a Birmingham motel where civil rights leaders were staying on May 14, 1963.

NO MORE BIRMINGHAMS

◀ *"No More Birminghams" reads the banner carried by Christian marchers in Washington, D.C., in September 1963.*

SOURCE EXPLORED

Marchers from All Souls Church in Washington, D.C., protest the killing of four African-American girls in Birmingham. The bomb planted in the Sixteenth Street Baptist Church exploded on Sunday, September 15, 1963, as youngsters were entering the basement to hear a sermon. It had been planted by members of the Ku Klux Klan. The reaction in the United States and further afield was one of revulsion. Many people saw the atrocity as evidence they had not taken opposition to civil rights seriously enough. Others blamed the governor of Alabama, George Wallace, for encouraging segregationists. Martin Luther King told him he had "blood on his hands."

KING'S LETTER

Martin Luther King was arrested on Good Friday 1963 as he marched with protesters in Birmingham. In jail, he wrote an open letter to white Alabama ministers who argued that civil rights should be pursued through the courts, not in the streets. King's letter defended his tactics, saying that the legal struggle and the protests could not be separated. The "Letter from Birmingham Jail" was published. It became increasingly popular as a manifesto for the whole civil rights movement.

THE MARCH ON WASHINGTON

▲ A group of African-American marchers carry signs protesting various aspects of civil rights, including school integration and improved housing.

In August 1963 around a quarter of a million people, largely middle-class black and white Americans, marched on Washington, D.C., to demand a civil rights bill. The march was the first time the major civil rights leaders all worked together. It was televised across the country and around the world. On the steps of the Lincoln Memorial, Martin Luther King Jr. made his memorable "I have a dream" speech.

▼ *The march ended in a huge rally on the National Mall in front of the Lincoln Memorial.*

SOURCE EXPLORED

This photograph shows the huge numbers of people who turned out for the March on Washington for Jobs and Freedom on August 28, 1963. No one had expected such large numbers. The crowd was notably diverse: old and young, men and women, and black and white people. On the National Mall, the crowd listened to a series of speeches by civil rights leaders and songs by black and white performers.

Martin Luther King Jr. delivered his famous "I have a dream" speech on the steps of the Lincoln Memorial in Washington, D.C., on August 28, 1963:

“ I have a dream that one day this nation will rise up and live out the true meaning of its creed: 'We hold these truths to be self-evident: that all men are created equal.' I have a dream that one day on the red hills of Georgia the sons of former slaves and the sons of former slave owners will be able to sit down together at a table of brotherhood. I have a dream that one day even the state of Mississippi, a state sweltering with the heat of injustice and oppression, will be transformed into an oasis of freedom and justice. I have a dream that my four children will one day live in a nation where they will not be judged by the color of their skin but by the content of their character. I have a dream today. ”

TROUBLE IN MISSISSIPPI

Mississippi emerged as a flashpoint in the civil rights struggle. In June 1963, a white racist shot and killed the NAACP field secretary Medgar Evers, who was trying to desegregate the University of Mississippi. Meanwhile, only just over 5 percent of African Americans in the state could vote. The average elsewhere in the South was 30 percent. The SNCC sent volunteers from the North to help register African Americans to vote. In summer 1964, called "Freedom Summer," segregationists shocked America when they murdered three young volunteers, two of whom were white.

◀ The family of civil rights worker Medgar Evers visit his grave in 1964 together with two thousand NAACP convention delegates.

MISSING CALL FBI

THE FBI IS SEEKING INFORMATION CONCERNING THE DISAPPEARANCE AT PHILADELPHIA, MISSISSIPPI, OF THESE THREE INDIVIDUALS ON JUNE 21, 1964. EXTENSIVE INVESTIGATION IS BEING CONDUCTED TO LOCATE GOODMAN, CHANEY, AND SCHWERNER, WHO ARE DESCRIBED AS FOLLOWS:

	ANDREW GOODMAN	JAMES EARL CHANEY	MICHAEL HENRY SCHWERNER

RACE:	White	Negro	White
SEX:	Male	Male	Male
DOB:	November 23, 1943	May 30, 1943	November 6, 1939
POB:	New York City	Meridian, Mississippi	New York City
AGE:	20 years	21 years	24 years
HEIGHT:	5'10"	5'7"	5'9" to 5'10"
WEIGHT:	150 pounds	135 to 140 pounds	170 to 180 pounds
HAIR:	Dark brown; wavy	Black	Brown
EYES:	Brown	Brown	Light blue
TEETH:		Good: none missing	
SCARS AND MARKS:		1 inch cut scar 2 inches above left ear.	Pock mark center of forehead, slight scar on bridge of nose, appendectomy scar, broken leg scar.

◀ *The Federal Bureau of Investigation (FBI) issued this poster during the search for the three missing men.*

THE GUILTY MEN

Baptist minister and Ku Klux Klan leader Edgar Ray Killen had ordered the murder of the volunteers. He was freed when a juror refused to convict him. Samuel Bowers, the Imperial Wizard of the Mississippi Klan, had been planning Schwerner's murder since the spring of 1964. Bowers was found guilty. In 2005, a grand jury charged Killen with the 1964 murders. This time he was sentenced to sixty years in jail.

SOURCE EXPLORED

This FBI Missing poster features the two CORE volunteers, Mickey Schwerner and James Chaney, and a volunteer college student, Andrew Goodman. The three men disappeared on June 21, 1964, after being arrested in Meridian, Mississippi. Investigators found their burned-out car on June 23 and launched a murder enquiry. In 1964, Mississippi was the only state without a central FBI office but agents arrived to investigate. The three men's bodies were found buried in a dam on August 4 following a tip-off. The FBI agents were blocked by local law enforcement agencies who tried to protect the FBI's suspects, including Edgar Ray Killen and Samuel Bowers. It required the intervention of the U.S. Supreme Court to force local courts to put the suspects on trial in 1967.

CIVIL RIGHTS AND THE WHITE HOUSE

Four presidents played a major part in introducing civil rights, starting with presidents Truman and Eisenhower in the 1950s. In the early 1960s, John F. Kennedy was criticized for being slow to join the movement, but he increased the number of African Americans in government. Lyndon B. Johnson, president from 1963 to 1969, wanted to make the country more equal. He introduced three major pieces of civil rights legislation. Some historians think Johnson's role in civil rights is often overlooked because of his controversial role in leading the United States into the Vietnam War in the mid-1960s.

◀ Lyndon B. Johnson believed that civil rights were an important part of fulfilling his vision of what he called the "Great Society."

President John F. Kennedy addressed the American people on June 11, 1963, to call for equal rights:

" This Nation was founded on the principle that all men are created equal, and that the rights of every man are diminished when the rights of one man are threatened... The heart of the question is whether all Americans are to be afforded equal rights and equal opportunities, whether we are going to treat our fellow Americans as we want to be treated. If an American, because his skin is dark, cannot eat lunch in a restaurant open to the public, if he cannot send his children to the best public school available, if he cannot vote for the public officials who will represent him, if, in short, he cannot enjoy the full and free life which all of us want, then who among us would be content to have the color of his skin changed and stand in his place? "

▲ President John F. Kennedy (right) meets civil rights leaders in the White House before the March on Washington in 1963.

SOURCE EXPLORED

President John F. Kennedy (right) meets organizers of the March on Washington, including Martin Luther King (second from left), in the White House. Kennedy had a small majority in Congress, and so was cautious about pushing civil rights legislation in case he lost Southern support. However, he appointed a record fifty African Americans to serve in his administration. They included federal judges, ambassadors, and assistant White House press secretary Andrew T. Hatcher. Kennedy also gave the Civil Rights Commission greater powers.

THE CIVIL RIGHTS ACT

▲ Senators in favor of the civil rights bill celebrate its passage on June 10, 1964. In the front are two leading supporters, Everett Dirksen (left) and Hubert Humphrey.

In July 1964, President Johnson signed the Civil Rights Bill into law. The bill allowed the federal government to use any legal means to end segregation in the South. It prohibited racial discrimination in public places and furthered school desegregation. Johnson worked hard to win over Southern support in Congress. The work of the African-American activists was now impossible for America to ignore.

◀ *With Martin Luther King behind him, President Johnson signs the Civil Rights Act into law in front of a national TV audience on July 2, 1964.*

SOURCE EXPLORED

On July 2, 1964, President Johnson signed the Civil Rights Act into law. It was ten years since the landmark ruling in *Brown v. Board of Education* and followed a decade of sustained civil rights lobbying. Johnson had previously served as the chairman of President Kennedy's Committee on Equal Employment Opportunities and had introduced a civil rights act in 1957. After Kennedy was killed in November 1963, the new president vowed to carry out Kennedy's proposals for reform, which he argued would be a fitting tribute. Johnson faced stiff opposition in the House but his savvy political skills helped gain Senate approval. Johnson used seventy-five pens to sign the bill, which were given away. One of the first was given to Martin Luther King, Jr.

GREAT SOCIETY

Often compared with President Franklin D. Roosevelt's New Deal, the Great Society was a series of programs launched by President Johnson between 1964 and 1965. Johnson aimed to end poverty and racial inequality. He wanted to improve education and healthcare for every American, regardless of their color. He introduced welfare payments, raised money for the arts and, like Roosevelt, wanted to protect the environment.

MARCH IN SELMA

In March 1965, civil rights organizations called for a march from Selma, Alabama, to the state capital, Montgomery, to call for a voting act. Despite the Civil Rights Act, many African Americans in the South still could not vote. State troopers attacked the marchers with clubs and tear gas. The march led to President Johnson introducing the Voting Rights Act later in the year .

▼ Protestors carry American flags after the march was finally allowed to leave Selma for Montgomery.

SOURCE EXPLORED

Martin Luther King, Jr. (left) and Ralph Abernathy, his associate in the Southern Christian Leadership Conference, walk at the head of the march from Selma to Montgomery on March 9, 1965. After being turned back by police, civil rights leaders petitioned for court protection for the marchers. The federal district court agreed. The 3,200 marchers finally set off for Montgomery on March 21 and reached the capital four days later. Less than five months later, President Johnson signed into law the Voting Rights Act.

▲ *Reverend Ralph Abernathy (right) studies the newspaper as he and Martin Luther King lead the attempted march.*

President Johnson addressed Congress on March 15, 1965, after the attacks on the Selma March. He explained why his Voting Rights Act was so vital to America:

" This time, on this issue, there must be no delay, or no hesitation, or no compromise with our purpose. We cannot, we must not, refuse to protect the right of every American to vote in every election that he may desire to participate in... But even if we pass this bill, the battle will not be over. What happened in Selma is part of a far larger movement which reaches into every section and state of America... The real hero of this struggle is the American Negro. His actions and protests, his courage to risk safety and even to risk his life, have awakened the conscience of this nation. His demonstrations have been designed to stir reform. He has called upon us to make good the promise of America. **"**

RACE RIOTS

The struggle for equal rights was concentrated in the South, but African Americans everywhere faced discrimination. Living in ghettos of poor quality apartments, they often struggled to earn a living. Their resentment boiled over into violence in Harlem in the summer of 1964. The following year, Watts in Los Angeles burned as African Americans rioted. Every summer until 1968, riots broke out in black ghettos across the country. A shocked President Johnson set up the Kerner Commission to try to understand what made African Americans turn to violence.

▶ *Police beat an African American during riots in Harlem in July 1964. Race riots became a regular feature of that summer.*

SOURCE EXPLORED

African-American protestors pass a police officer on the streets of Harlem. They hold photographs of police lieutenant Thomas Gilligan, who on July 16, 1964, shot dead fifteen-year-old African American James Powell. The police said Powell and other boys had been causing trouble on Manhattan's Upper East Side. A protest march degenerated into violence. Riots raged in Harlem and Bedford-Stuyvesant for six nights. Violence spread to other cities in the summer, including Philadelphia and Chicago. In September, a grand jury cleared Gilligan of any crime. He claimed Powell charged him with a knife; the claim was disputed by some of the witnesses.

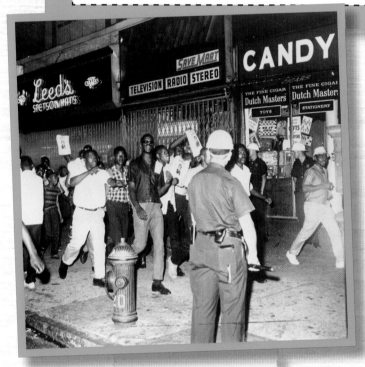

▲ Protestors carrying photographs of Lieutenant Gilligan march along 125th Street in Harlem.

AS THEY SAW IT

"Our nation is moving toward two societies, one black, one white—separate and unequal.... What white Americans have never fully understood—but what the Negro can never forget—is that... white institutions created [the ghetto], white institutions maintain it, and white society condones [supports] it."

—Kerner Commission Report on the riots in Northern cities, February 1968

RADICAL ORGANIZATIONS

During the 1960s, more radical groups joined the campaign for civil rights. They included the Nation of Islam (NOI), which had originally been formed in 1930 as an alternative to Christianity. In the 1950s its outspoken spokesman Malcolm X rejected all integration with whites. He quit the NOI in 1964 and was killed by NOI extremists a year later. In 1966, Huey P. Newton and Bobby Seale founded the Black Panthers as a global, nonwhite, working-class organization. They argued that black Americans were justified in using violence in pursuit of social equality.

◄ *Malcolm X's rejection of integration into white society led him to quit the Nation of Islam. NOI members shot him dead on February 21, 1965.*

On March 12, 1964, Malcolm X told a press conference about his idea of "black nationalism." His radical views led him to split from the Nation of Islam the following year.

" Whites can help us but they can't join us. There can be no black–white unity until there is first black unity. There can be no workers' solidarity until there is first some racial solidarity. We cannot think of uniting with others, until after we have first united among ourselves... Concerning nonviolence: it is criminal to teach a man not to defend himself when he is the constant victim of brutal attacks. It is legal and lawful to own a shotgun or a rifle... We should be peaceful, law-abiding—but the time has come for the American Negro to fight back in self-defense whenever and wherever he is being unjustly and unlawfully attacked. "

▲ Black Panthers stage a mass demonstration on the steps of a courthouse in New York City.

SOURCE EXPLORED

Black Panthers give the "black power" salute outside a New York court where members of the party are on trial for a bomb plot in 1971. The party's program of community work made it popular, but it also argued that violence was necessary to achieve improved equality for blacks. Its members wore a militaristic uniform of leather jackets and black berets. The clenched-fist salute was a popular sign of black radicalism in the 1970s.

THE ASSASSINATION OF MARTIN LUTHER KING

On April 4, 1968, Martin Luther King Jr. was shot as he stood on the balcony of his motel in Memphis, Tennessee. The killing was later blamed on a white racist. King was in Memphis to support striking black sanitation workers. The strike had become increasingly violent. After King's murder, riots broke out in more than 130 cities, including Washington, D.C.

▼ *Demonstrators pushing for more action on civil rights protest outside the White House after King's death in April 1968.*

SOURCE EXPLORED

Flowers and tributes mark the site of King's death. King often stayed in the same room (306) at the Lorraine Motel in Memphis, Tennessee. On the evening of April 4, 1968, he was standing on the balcony outside his room when he was shot by James Earl Ray. King died later that evening in hospital. The night before, King had made a speech at the Mason Temple in Memphis. He told the congregation that he did not fear death and was happy with whatever happened to him. King had been the target of many assassination attempts over the years. Likening the eventual achievement of equal rights to arriving in the promised land, he told his listeners, "I may not get there with you."

JAMES EARL RAY

On June 8, 1968, two months after the shooting, James Earl Ray was arrested as he arrived at Heathrow Airport in England. He was sent back to Tennessee and charged with King's murder. Ray was already a convicted criminal and a known segregationist. He confessed to killing King and was sentenced to ninety-nine years in jail. He died in jail in 1998. Many people, including King's family, have long believed that Ray was not the real killer.

◀ In the days after the shooting, followers turned the balcony where King had stood into a shrine.

43

TIMELINE

1948	**July 26:** President Truman signs Executive Order 9981, outlawing discrimination in the armed services.
1954	**May 17:** The Supreme Court ruling in Brown v. Board of Education of Topeka, Kansas (Brown v. Board of Education) that segregation in public schools is unconstitutional.
1955	**August:** A fourteen-year-old African American, Emmett Till, is beaten and killed in Mississippi for allegedly whistling at a white woman. His killers are acquitted by an all-white jury. The case outrages many Americans.
	December 1: Rosa Parks refuses to give up her seat on a bus in Montgomery, Alabama. The black community launches a bus boycott that lasts over a year.
1957	**February:** African American ministers found the Southern Christian Leadership Convention, with Martin Luther King Jr. as president.
	September 4: There are violent clashes when nine African American students try to attend Central High School in Little Rock, Arkansas. President Johnson sends federal troops to enforce integration.
1960	**February 1:** African American students begin a sit-in at the lunch counter of Woolworth in Greensboro, North Carolina, to protest segregation. The sit-in movement spreads around the country. Woolworth integrates its lunch counters six months later.
	April: The Student Nonviolent Coordinating Committee (SNCC) is founded at Shaw University, North Carolina.
1961	**May 4:** Student volunteers begin a program of "freedom rides" through the South in a program organized by CORE and SNCC. Many of the thousand volunteers face attack by racist mobs.
1962	**October 1:** The enrollment of James Meredith as the first black student at the University of Mississippi causes such violence that President Kennedy sends five thousand troops to the campus.
1963	**April 16:** Martin Luther King Jr. is arrested during protests in Birmingham, Alabama; he writes his "Letter from Birmingham Jail," which becomes a manifesto for the civil rights movement.

May: *Police brutality during ongoing protests in Birmingham gains widespread sympathy for the civil rights movement.*

June 12: *NAACP activist Medgar Evers is murdered outside his home in Jackson, Mississippi.*

August 28: *Some 250,000 people join the March on Washington to call for civil rights; Martin Luther King delivers his speech "I have a dream."*

September 15: *Four young African-American girls are killed by a bomb attack on the Sixteenth Street Baptist Church in Birmingham, Alabama.*

1964

January: *The Twenty-Fourth Amendment abolishes a poll tax which had been a barrier to African American voting in the South. Civil rights groups organize "Freedom Summer," in which volunteers urge blacks to register to vote.*

July 2: *President Lyndon B. Johnson signs the Civil Rights Act.*

August 4: *FBI investigators find the bodies of three civil rights volunteers who have been murdered by the Ku Klux Klan in Mississippi.*

1965

February 21: *Radical leader Malcolm X is murdered by members of the Nation of Islam.*

March 7: *Police injure fifty peaceful protestors as they turn back a march from Selma to Montgomery in Alabama in support of voting rights.*

August 10: *The Voting Rights Act lifts restrictions on black voters in the South.*

August 11: *Race riots break out in Watts, Los Angeles.*

1966

October: *Huey P. Newton and Bobby Seale found the Black Panthers in California.*

1968

April 4: *Martin Luther King is shot dead in Memphis, Tennessee. Convicted racist James Earl Ray is later found guilty of his murder.*

April 11: *President Johnson signs a new civil rights act that outlaws discrimination in housing.*

GLOSSARY

activist A person who campaigns for social change.

atrocity An act of evil that causes great revulsion.

boycott To cease buying goods or services from a supplier as a protest.

civil rights The rights enjoyed by all citizens to political and social freedom and equality.

communism A political system based on a lack of private ownership.

constitutional Permitted under the terms of the constitution.

desegregation The elimination of differences in the treatment of different races.

discrimination The unfair treatment of different groups of people on the grounds of race, sex, or other qualities.

Executive Order An order issued by the President that has the force of law.

freshmen Students in their first year of high school or college.

ghetto A poor part of a city occupied by an ethnic minority group.

integrated Having no difference in the treatment of different races.

lobbying Seeking to influence a legislator or politician about an issue.

lynch For a mob to kill someone unlawfully, especially by hanging.

manifesto A document laying out a political program.

nonviolence The use of peaceful means rather than force to achieve social change.

oppression Prolonged, cruel treatment of someone.

oratory Skill in public speaking; someone with the skill is called an orator.

picket To stand outside a venue as a form of protest.

placard A printed or handwritten sign for public display.

revenue The money raised by a business or organization.

seamstress Someone who sews and repairs garments.

segregation The separation of a group of people from others, particularly on the basis of race.

sit-in A peaceful protest in which protestors occupy a place and refuse to leave until their demands are met.

vigil A period of prayer or keeping watch, particularly during the night.

FURTHER INFORMATION

Books

Herr, Melody. *Sitting for Equal Service: Lunch Counter Sit-Ins, United States, 1960s.* Civil Rights Struggles Around the World. Minneapolis, MN: Twenty-First Century Books, 2010.

Mannheimer, Ann S. *Martin Luther King, Jr.* Trailblazer Biographies. Minneapolis, MN: Carolrhoda Books, 2005.

Mortensen, Lori. *Voices of the Civil Rights Marches: A Primary Source Exploration of the Struggle for Racial Equality.* We Shall Overcome. North Mankato, MN: Capstone Press, 2015.

Price, Sean. *When Will I Get In? Segregation and Civil Rights.* American History Through Primary Sources. Chicago, Il: Raintree, 2007.

Schlepper, Bill. *The Mississippi Burning Trial: A Primary Source Account.* Great Trials of the 20th Century. New York: Rosen Publishing Group.

Spilsbury, Richard. *The Civil Rights Movement: The 20th Century.* Primary Source Readers. Chicago, IL: Heinemann Library, 2014.

Websites

civilrightsmuseum.org
Overview of the struggle for civil rights from the Civil Rights Museum in Memphis, Tennessee.

www.ducksters.com/history/civil_rights/african-american_civil_rights_movement.php
Ducksters.com page about the civil rights movement.

www.history.com/topics/black-history/civil-rights-movement
History.com analysis of the civil rights movement, with videos and links.

memory.loc.gov/ammem/aaohtml/exhibit/aointro.html
Library of Congress history of African Americans, ending with the civil rights movement.

Publisher's note to educators and parents: Our editors have carefully reviewed these websites to ensure that they are suitable for students. Many websites change frequently, however, and we cannot guarantee that a site's future contents will continue to meet our high standards of quality and educational value. Be advised that students should be closely supervised whenever they access the Internet.

INDEX